First Printing, 2024

ISBN for Print Editions (979-8-8692-6575-3)

ISBN for Electronic Editions (979-8-8692-6576-0)

Forward By Travis Johnson:

Purpose, Power, Profit

I had the pleasure of meeting Richard Kaufman in 2019. Richard invited me to be a guest on his original podcast while I was studying at the Naval War College in Newport, Rhode Island.

I had been doing some nonprofit work; helped raise $500,000; served on the board of the SHINE Foundation; and was Vice President of **Books by Vets**. I knew Richard was genuine, caring, and a little weird from that first interview. We hit it off immediately!

Later that year, Richard and others encouraged me to start the Nonprofit Architect Podcast. It was a hit and we ranked #4 in the U.S. within 3 months of launching. We quickly reached 18,000 downloads, hit the top 10 in 8 countries, and were downloaded in 90+ countries.

I received dozens of messages wanting to know how I was able to accomplish so much in such a short period with no experience or established audience. I wrote the Ultimate Podcast Guide; and Richard bought the first copy!

Richard messaged me and shared that, although he had been podcasting for 3 years, I had tripled his downloads.

Even though Richard had far more experience than I, he recognized there might be a few things I was doing that could help him grow.

This is who Richard is.

He is dedicated to his craft, identifies there is room for improvement, and is willing to be humble in his pursuit.

He's willing to ask for guidance and mentorship from podcast titans like John Lee Dumas, host of Entrepreneurs on Fire, and newbies like me, Travis Johnson host of the Nonprofit Architect Podcast and Titan Evolution Podcast.

If you're reading this and don't know Richard; here's all you need to know: Richard Kaufman is my brother. He is raw, authentic, and genuinely wants everyone to win!

I love you, brother. Keep the faith and I look forward to meeting you in person.

Travis Johnson

THE PODCASTING BLUEPRINT: MASTERING PURPOSE, POWER AND PROFIT..

How we hit over 2 Million downloads

RICHARD KAUFMAN

The Podcasting Blueprint:

Mastering Purpose, Power, and Profit

by

Richard Kaufman

Opening Quote:

Richard Kaufman is the epitome of podcast-based media.

The evolution of radio into podcasts gave entrepreneurs the ability to create home-based global media centered around their brand.

Rich shocked the world with his perseverance, humility, and love for his fellow veterans.

I can think of no better person to teach you the process of podcasting than a man that reached over a million downloads.

- Dr. Rob Garcia, Founder, Shift Magazine.

PREFACE:

Welcome to "**The Podcasting Blueprint: Mastering Purpose, Power, and Profit**", a journey from obscurity to prominence, from uncertainty to clarity, and from dreams to reality.

I am so grateful for you.

When I started, I was lost and didn't know where to start. I spent over $50,000 and thousands of hours reading, studying, watching YouTube® to learn everything I am teaching in this book.

And I made PLENTY of mistakes, as you will learn.

This is not just another guide; it is a testament to the power of resilience, strategy, and authenticity in the digital age.

My story is improbable — a ninth-grade dropout stepping into the vast, unforgiving world of digital content, with no formal business or marketing education.

Yet, it is a story that underscores a universal truth: success is not about the credentials you hold, but about the lessons you learn and the actions you take.

When I started my podcasting journey, I was armed with nothing but a burning desire to share my voice, to bring untold stories to light, and to connect with like-minded individuals across the globe.

The path was fraught with challenges and setbacks, each one teaching me more about the medium, the market, and, most importantly, myself.

"**The Podcasting Blueprint: Mastering Purpose, Power, and Profit**" is the culmination of all those lessons — a comprehensive guide designed to take you from the concept of a podcast to the reality of a thriving digital platform.

Whether you are an aspiring podcaster, a seasoned content creator, or simply someone curious about the mechanics of success in podcasting, this book is for you.

In these pages, you will find not just technical guidelines and marketing strategies but also personal anecdotes and insights that illuminate the human element of podcasting.

You will learn how to find your unique voice, engage with your audience on a deeper level, and turn your passion into a profitable venture.

This book is a blueprint, yes, but it is also a call to action: to pursue your passions, to speak your truth, and to create content that resonates and inspires.

Join me on this journey, and let's unlock the full potential of your podcasting venture together.

Here's to your success, to the power of your voice, and to the exciting journey ahead.

Let's Roll,

Your Coach

Richard Kaufman

TABLE OF CONTENTS

The Podcasting Blueprint: Mastering Purpose, Power, And Profit.

How We Hit Over 2,000,000 Downloads.

- Exploring cross-media opportunities (like YouTube, blogs)

10. **Course Conclusion**
    - Recap of key learnings
    - Action plan for starting a podcast
    - Resources for further learning

11. **Bonus Materials**
    - Checklists and templates
    - Interviews with successful podcasters
    - Access to a community forum for ongoing support

Chapter 1

Chapter One: The Podcasting Phenomenon...

Introduction:

In the digital age, the art of storytelling and information sharing has evolved remarkably, giving rise to a unique and powerful medium: podcasting.

This book is dedicated to unraveling the intricacies of podcasting, a platform that has transformed the way we consume audio content.

The Genesis and Growth of Podcasting...

Podcasting, essentially a blend of 'iPod' and 'broadcasting', emerged in the early 2000s as a revolutionary way for creators to distribute audio content over the internet.

Initially a niche medium, it has since burgeoned into a global phenomenon, with millions of podcasts available on various themes and subjects.

This book will explore the historical journey of podcasting, highlighting key milestones and the evolution of technology that fueled its growth.

Understanding the Podcasting Landscape...

Podcasting encompasses a diverse range of topics, from educational content and storytelling to news and entertainment.

This book will provide an overview of the different genres of podcasts, popular platforms for hosting and listening, and insights into the demographics of podcast listeners and creators.

The Benefits of Podcasting...

Podcasting offers numerous advantages, both to content creators and listeners.

For creators, it provides an accessible platform for storytelling, sharing knowledge, and building communities.

For listeners, podcasts offer convenience, a variety of content, and the opportunity to learn and be entertained "on the go".

This book will delve into these benefits in detail, highlighting real-world examples and success stories.

Challenges in the World of Podcasting…

Despite its advantages, podcasting also presents several challenges.

These include issues related to content discovery, monetization, maintaining listener engagement, and technical aspects like audio quality and distribution.

This book will discuss these challenges and explore strategies that successful podcasters have employed to overcome them.

The Future of Podcasting…

As we conclude this book, we will speculate on the future of podcasting.

This will include emerging trends, the potential impact of new technologies like AI and virtual reality, and how podcasting might evolve in the coming years.

With this comprehensive in-depth look into the world of podcasting, we set the stage for a deeper exploration into the world of podcasting, a medium that continues to captivate and engage audiences worldwide.

Hopefully you are excited as I was to write this!

Chapter 2: Starting Your Podcast - Finding Your Niche and Target Audience...

Finding Your Niche...

- Identifying your podcast's niche is crucial.

- It's about finding a subject you are passionate about and that interests others.

- Start by listing topics you are knowledgeable about or want to explore.

- Then, research to see if there is an audience for these topics. Consider checking existing podcasts in similar areas to understand their approach and audience engagement.

Understanding Your Target Audience..

Once your niche is clear, understand who your target audience is.

Are they young professionals, hobbyists, parents, or students?

Knowing your audience helps you tailor your content to their interests. This increases engagement and loyalty.

Use tools like social media analytics and surveys to gather insights about your audience's preferences.

Cultivating Ideas...

Ideas are the lifeblood of your podcast. Keep a journal or digital document to jot down ideas as they come.

Regularly brainstorm topics, guests, and unique angles to approach your subject.

Listening to other podcasts and reading widely can also inspire new ideas.

Setting Up Your Recording Space...

Your recording environment impacts the quality of your podcast.

Choose a quiet, echo-free room. Simple soundproofing can be done using bookshelves, carpets, and curtains.

Ensure your space is comfortable, since you'll be spending a lot of time there.

Essential Equipment and Software...

1. Microphone..,

Invest in a good-quality microphone. It doesn't have to be expensive but should capture clear, crisp sound.

2. Headphones…

Good headphones are essential for monitoring your audio quality.

3. Recording Software…

Many free and paid options are available. Audacity and GarageBand are popular choices for beginners.

4. Editing Software…

Quality editing can transform your podcast. Adobe Audition, Hindenburg Journalist, and Audacity are excellent choices.

5. Hosting Platform…

Select a hosting platform to distribute your podcast. Options include Podbean, Anchor, and Buzzsprout.

6. Miscellaneous…

Consider pop filters, microphone stands, and acoustic panels for better sound quality.

Conclusion…

Starting a podcast requires thoughtful planning — from finding your niche to setting up your recording space.

Invest time in understanding your audience and cultivating engaging content.

Remember, quality equipment and software are crucial; but your passion and consistency are what will truly make your podcast stand out.

We will be going into detail in the upcoming chapters. We are here to make sure you succeed.

Chapter 3

Chapter 3: Crafting the Perfect Podcast

Don't Get Too Wrapped Around The Axle! Just Start!

1. Basics of Recording a Podcast..

To start recording a podcast, you need a quiet, echo-free environment, I record in our home studio in the basement.

Consider a room with carpeting and soft furnishings to absorb sound. Setting up your microphone is key.

Choose a cardioid microphone for its ability to capture sound from the front while minimizing background noise.

Position the microphone at mouth level, about six inches away, to capture clear, consistent audio.

Use a shock mount to reduce vibrations and a pop filter to minimize plosives (hard 'p' and 'b' sounds that seem to "pop" in the mic).

2. Tips for High-Quality Audio…

High-quality audio hinges on both equipment and technique.

First, ensure your microphone is of good quality; it doesn't have to be expensive, just reliable, more expensive does not mean that it will perform better. I like the **Rode PodMic Cardioid Dynamic Broadcast Microphone**.

When recording, speak directly into the mic with a steady, clear voice. Keep the recording levels below 0 dB (decibels) to avoid peaking and distortion.

Use noise reduction techniques: close windows and doors, turn off fans or air conditioners, and use a noise gate to eliminate background noise. Properly positioning your microphone can also greatly reduce unwanted sounds.

3. Editing Techniques and Software Recommendations…

Editing is where your podcast comes to life. Start by removing any mistakes or long pauses or ums or words you find yourself repeating over and over.

Software like Audacity (free), Adobe Audition (subscription-based), and GarageBand (for Mac users) are excellent choices.

Use equalization (EQ) to balance the tone, making your voice sound warm and clear.

I never really used these but a lot of people love them.

Compression is crucial for leveling your audio — ensuring consistency in volume.

I use Streamyard and their audio quality is truly amazing.

For beginners, Audacity offers a user-friendly interface, while Adobe Audition is suitable for those seeking more advanced features.

4. Adding Music, Effects, and Closed Captions...

Enhance your podcast with music and sound effects. Use royalty-free music as an intro, outro, or during transitions.

I had our intro video professionally made by William Maitre and our outtro was made by Michael Dolbow who is an amazing voice actor.

Websites like Free Music Archive or Jamendo offer a vast selection.

When integrating music, ensure it doesn't overpower your voice; keep it subtle in the background.

Sound effects can add personality but use them sparingly to avoid distraction.

To make your podcast accessible, add closed captions. 80 percent of people who watch YouTube® or short-form videos watch them with the sound off.

I also use the Headliner and Auto CC apps for making one- to three-minute clips of each show.

Services like Rev or Amara can transcribe your podcast, which you can then edit for accuracy.

Key Takeaways...

- **Recording Setup:** Quiet space, proper microphone setup, and soundproofing techniques.

- **Audio Quality:** Use a good microphone, speak clearly, and manage recording levels.

Editing: Choose the right software, remove unnecessary parts, and use EQ and compression.

- **Enhancements:** Add music and effects judiciously and include closed captions for accessibility.

By following these steps, you can produce a podcast that not only sounds professional but also engages and retains your audience through quality content and production.

Chapter 4: Branding and Identity

Designing Your Podcast and Logo Art...

Creating a visually captivating logo and podcast art is crucial in establishing your brand identity.

Your logo is often the first thing potential listeners see, so it must embody your podcast's essence and appeal to your target audience. Here are key elements to consider:

Understand Your Brand...

What is the central theme of your podcast?

Whom are you speaking to?

Visual Elements...

Choose colors that reflect your podcast's mood and theme.

Select a font that complements your brand's personality.

Use images or symbols that resonate with your content and audience.

Simplicity and Memorableness...

- A simple, clean design is often more memorable and easily recognizable.

- Avoid clutter and overly complex designs.

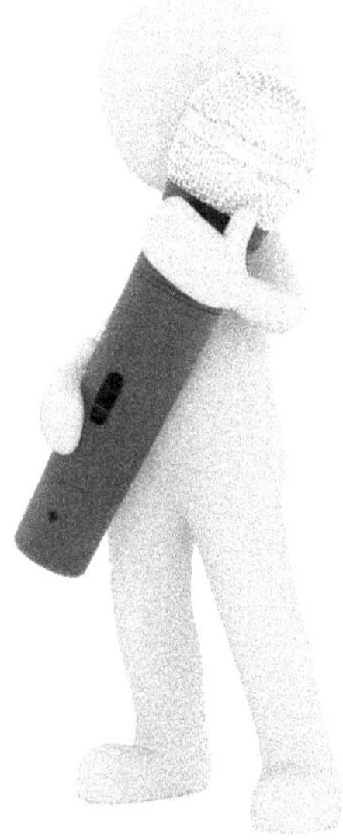

Crafting a Compelling Podcast Description...

Your podcast description is a brief yet powerful tool for attracting listeners. It should be engaging, informative, and reflective of what your podcast offers.

Use a catchy opening line that grabs attention.

Clearly outline what your podcast covers.

Highlight what makes your podcast different.

Language and Tone...

Ensure the description aligns with your podcast's tone – whether it's formal, casual, humorous, or serious.

Use keywords that potential listeners might search for.

Call to Action...

Encourage listeners to subscribe or tune in to the next episode.

Develop a Unique and Consistent Style...

A unique and consistent style sets your podcast apart and builds listener loyalty. This includes not just the visual elements, but also the tone and structure of your content.

Tone of Voice...

Consistency in your tone of voice helps in forming a connection with your audience.

Whether it's authoritative, conversational, or playful, stick to a tone that reflects your brand.

Content Structure...

Regular segments or recurring themes can provide a familiar structure for your audience.

Consistency in episode length and release schedule also contributes to a reliable listener experience.

Engaging with Listeners...

Interaction with your audience, such as Q&A sessions, can personalize the experience and strengthen your community.

In conclusion, a strong brand identity for your podcast involves a thoughtful blend of visual and content elements.

Your logo and podcast art, description, and consistent style play a pivotal role in attracting and retaining your audience.

By focusing on these aspects, you can create a memorable and distinctive brand that stands out in the ever-growing podcast landscape.

Chapter 5: Publishing and Distributing Your Podcast…

Choosing a Podcast Platform…

When you're ready to publish your podcast, the first step is choosing the right platform.

We have been using Spotify FKA (Formerly Known As) Anchor — (Spotify for Podcasters) — from day one.

A podcast platform is a service that hosts your audio files and makes them accessible to listeners through various distribution channels. **Some popular podcast hosting platforms include:**

Libsyn…

Renowned for its reliability and range of plans, Libsyn caters to both beginners and experienced podcasters.

Anchor Now Spotify…

Known for its free hosting services, Anchor also offers tools for recording and editing podcasts directly on the platform.

Their analytics are amazing, too, and they also distribute to many different platforms.

Podbean…

With unlimited hosting services, Podbean is also user-friendly and offers monetization opportunities.

Each platform has its own set of features, like analytics, marketing tools, and monetization options, so it's important to choose one that fits your needs and goals.

Distributing Your Podcast to Platforms like Apple, Spotify, and Others…

After choosing a hosting platform, the next step is to distribute your podcast to popular listening platforms like Apple Podcasts, Spotify, Google Podcasts, and others.

Here's a basic overview of how to do this:

Submit to Apple Podcasts…

Create an Apple ID, log in to iTunes Connect, and submit your podcast's RSS feed for approval.

Most people listen to podcasts on iTunes. Don't leave any money on the table.

Distribute to Spotify…

Most hosting platforms offer a direct way to submit your podcast to Spotify. Check your host's dashboard for this option.

Google Podcasts…

<u>Google Podcasts</u> automatically fetches podcasts from the web, but you can also directly submit your feed for faster indexing.

Remember, each platform has its own set of guidelines and approval processes, so it's important to familiarize yourself with them.

Understanding RSS Feeds...

An RSS (Really Simple Syndication) feed is crucial for podcast distribution. It is a file that contains your podcast's information — episodes, titles, descriptions, etc.

When you upload a new episode to your hosting platform, the RSS feed automatically updates and informs subscriber platforms of the new content.

Here's what you need to understand about RSS feeds:

Creation...

Your podcast hosting platform usually generates an RSS feed for you.

Consistency...

Ensure your feed URL remains the same. Changing it can lead to losing subscribers.

Content Updates...

Whenever you publish a new episode, it's automatically added to your RSS feed and distributed to subscribed platforms.

Links for Further Learning...

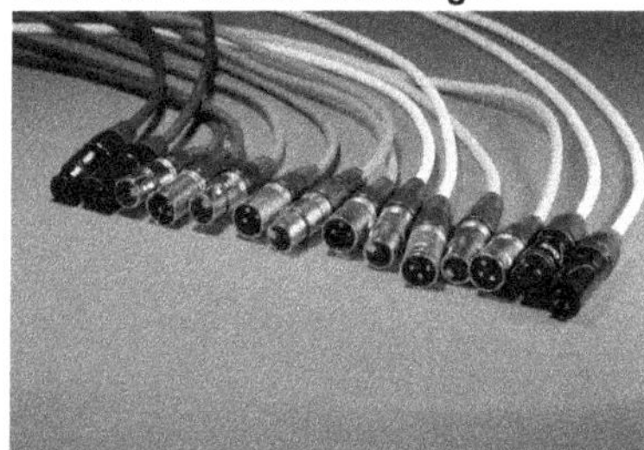

Choosing a Platform...

For a deeper comparison of podcast platforms, visit <u>PodcastInsights</u> for their latest reviews.

Distributing Your Podcast...

Check out <u>The Podcast Host</u> for a detailed guide on distributing your podcast across various platforms.

Understanding RSS Feeds...

For more on RSS feeds, visit <u>Transistor's Guide</u> on understanding and managing your podcast's RSS feed.

Remember, the world of podcasting is always evolving, so staying informed and adaptable is key to your success.

You can always reach out to us at Vertical Momentum Podcast.

Chapter 6

Chapter 6: Monetizing Your Podcast

Now The Fun Begins…

How to Get Sponsorships…

We Have Over 20 Paying Sponsors On The Vertical Momentum Resiliency Podcast Using These Steps…

To attract sponsors and advertisers, you need to understand and communicate your podcast's value proposition clearly.

This includes your listener demographics, engagement rates, and unique selling points. All of these can be found in your show's analytics.

Creating a Media Kit…

Develop a professional media kit that showcases your podcast's statistics, audience demographics, and success stories. This kit serves as your business card to potential sponsors. Tammi Moses created ours. Thank you, sis.

Identifying Potential Sponsors…

Look for companies and brands that align with your podcast's theme and audience. Ours Is Veterans, First Responders, and Entrepreneurs.

Tailor your pitch to show how sponsoring your podcast can benefit them. ALWAYS lead with value.

Negotiating Deals…

Understanding the market rates for podcast advertising and be prepared to negotiate terms that are beneficial for both you and the sponsor. We can definitely help with this.

Membership and Subscription Models…

Setting Up a Membership Platform…

Platforms like Patreon or Memberful can be used to create membership tiers offering exclusive content, early access, or special perks to subscribers. Buy Me a Cup of Coffee is amazing too.

Benefits of Subscriptions…

The advantages of having a steady, predictable income stream can help in the consistent production of content. The more you can pay to advertise the more value you can bring to the world.

Offer exclusive content for your subscribers. iTunes and Spotify now offer these for your listeners.

Engaging with Subscribers…

Offer engaging and unique content to your subscribers.

This could include behind-the-scenes content, Q&A sessions, or members-only episodes. Spotify also offers polls you can use for each episode.

Promotion Strategies…

Promote your membership program on your podcast and other social media platforms.

Highlight the benefits of joining and provide easy access links.

Mention them in the episode and also put links in the liner notes.

Merchandising and Crowdfunding…

Developing Merchandise…

We offer t shirts, hats, swag, coffee, and our Top-Selling book on our website Vertical Momentum Podcast.

Create and sell podcast-themed merchandise such as t-shirts, mugs, or stickers.

These items can strengthen your brand and provide an additional revenue stream.

Choosing the Right Merchandising Platform…

Platforms like Teespring or Shopify can be used for merchandising.

We choose to use a Veteran company to do all of our swag https://www.reallydesigns.biz/verticalmomentum

Crowdfunding for Specific Projects…

Platforms like Kickstarter or Indiegogo can be used for raising funds for specific projects, such as upgrading equipment or funding a special series.

Engaging the Audience in Crowdfunding…

Share your crowdfunding campaign with your audience and explain how their support will enhance the podcast's quality or content.

Affiliate Marketing…

My mentor John Lee Dumas taught me this hack — wow!

Understanding Affiliate Marketing…

Businesses will give you a link, so that podcasters like you and me can earn commissions by promoting products or services.

You can make a lot of money using affiliate marketing.

Look for businesses you love, go to their websites to see if they have affiliate links, and sign up.

This was a great article I found https://blog.hubspot.com/marketing/best-affiliate-programs

Choosing Affiliates Wisely…

Select affiliate products or services that align with your podcast's content, your values,you're your audience's interests.

For instance, I won't have an alcohol brand sponsoring us. People know I am in recovery soooo not a good look. LOL!

Disclosure and Trust…

It is very important to always be upfront and honest with your audience about your affiliate relationships to maintain trust.

Best Practices for Affiliate Promotion…

People know if I use it I will promote it.

Even when I was with GNC, I wouldn't recommend a product if I didn't have real-life experience with it.

Obviously I didn't pull all these things out of my butt. LOL!.

I've spent over $30,000 and hundreds of hours on courses and books from the likes of Gary Vee, John Lee Dumas (JLD), Erik Allen, Travis Johnson, and all the best podcasters in the world.

So, this chapter outline provides a comprehensive guide to monetizing a podcast, and covering various revenue streams from sponsorships to affiliate marketing.

Each section is designed to offer practical advice and strategies to help podcasters effectively monetize their content.

We Will always be here to support you. Just message us.

Chapter 7

Chapter 7: Marketing and Promotion…

In the competitive world of podcasting, creating great content isn't enough; you also need effective marketing and promotion strategies.

This chapter delves into key tactics like building a website, leveraging social media, collaborating with guests, and utilizing SEO to enhance your podcast's reach and audience engagement.

Building a Website and Email List…

Your podcast's website is the central hub for your content.

It provides a platform for listeners to discover more about your show, access episodes, and engage with supplementary content.

Our friend William Maitre built our website: www.verticalmomentumpodcast.com

Website Essentials…

Include an "About" page, Contact Information, Episode Archive, and a Blog for additional content.

Make sure that you have a very obvious "Call to Action" button so people can click it right then and there.

Email Lists…

Collect email addresses through sign-up forms on your website.

Use these lists to send regular updates, episode releases, and exclusive content, keeping your audience engaged and informed.

Make sure that you capture listeners' and guests' information. Make sure that you own your lists; so that, if you get shut out of any social media platform, you will still be able to get in touch with all your followers. OWN YOUR LIST, as I was taught by the amazing Russell Brunson.

We use Mailchimp and have for many years. It is easy to use even for a low-tech redneck like myself check it out at www.mailchimp.com.

Leveraging Social Media for Growth…

Social media platforms are invaluable for promoting your podcast.

Platform Selection…

Focus on platforms where your target audience is most active, be it Instagram®, X (formerly Twitter), Facebook®, LinkedIn®, or TikTok®.

We do most of our damage on LinkedIn® and Facebook® because that is where our ideal avatar spends time; but we have a presence on many other platforms including YouTube® because not everyone consumes content the same way.

Gary Vee says "If You Are Not Everywhere You Are Nowhere."

Content Strategy…

Share episode snippets, behind-the-scenes content. Engage with your audience through polls, Q&As, and live sessions.

We use Headliner for snippets and Auto CC to add captions to our videos because over 60% of people that are on YouTube® have the sound off?

Consistency and Scheduling…

When I was growing up I loved the A-Team and would be ready with my drinks and snacks at the time the **TV Guide** (YES I'm that old, LOL) would say it was on and, if it wasn't on, I'd be mad.

So pick a day and time that you can put out your show consistently.

Even if you're going to be on vacation, you can still schedule when your podcast goes out.

We don't want to make our listeners feel like I did when I missed seeing Mr. T on a Friday night!

Maintain a regular posting schedule to keep your audience engaged, if you don't they WILL leave.

Collaborations and Guest Appearances…

Collaborations can introduce your podcast to new audiences.

Guest Selection…

Invite guests who align with your podcast's theme and can bring value to your audience.

Make sure that they can provide real value to your audience and not just try to sell stuff, or you will lose all credibility.

Cross-Promotion…

Collaborate with other podcasters for guest appearances on each other's shows, tapping into each other's audiences.

The FASTEST way to grow an audience is to make guest appearances on other shows. We will make at least 250 appearances on others' shows this year.

IMPORTANT… make sure that when you have been on someone else's show, you leave a written review and publicly promote your episode with them, and tag them.

You know how hard you work. so treat others the way you want to be treated.

SEO Strategies for Podcasts…

SEO isn't just for websites; it's crucial for podcasts, too.

My brother Patrick Burt has been my SEO partner since day one.

At the time of this writing we have had over 1,500,000 downloads, ranked in the Top 0.5% of All Podcasts Globally according to Listen Notes, and are on the same lists as Gary Vee, Ed Mylett, Tim Ferris, and Jocko.

We also dominate the first 6 pages of Google using his teachings.

Keyword Optimization…

Use relevant keywords in your podcast title, description, and website content to improve visibility.

I use short-tail and long-tail keywords In our descriptions. For instance, our podcast talks about resilience, so I pick some short-tail keywords like resilience, mental health.

An example of a long-tail keyword would be something like "How do I take care of my mental health?" or "How do I build resilience?"

These are terms and questions that people are going to be putting into search engines. If you want to be found, your show and topics have to be searchable.

Transcripts…

Publish episode transcripts on your website to boost SEO and make your content accessible to a wider audience.

I'm old school, I listen to all my episodes, writing out notes, and the highlights. Then I give them to my assistant to write the transcripts, podcast descriptions, and liner notes.

If you don't have an assistant or the the money or time check out: www.happyscribe.com.

Backlinks…

Encourage guest speakers and collaborators to link back to your podcast from their websites and social media.

I also make sure that every guest sends me their links to put into the liner notes.

When I publish the episode, I email to all the guests the links to share, as I had them promise to do when they signed up.

I use www.calendly.com to book all my guests.

Additional Resources…

- For building a website, platforms like WordPress, Squarespace, and Wix offer user-friendly solutions.

We have a Wordpress blog very easy to set up.

- To learn more about email marketing, Mailchimp and ConvertKit provide valuable tools and guides.

- For social media strategies, HubSpot and Hootsuite offer extensive resources and courses. I definitely suggest working with my mentor Robert Garcia (The Warrior Strategist) for all your P.R and social media needs.

Here is a FREE resource! 📷 Look at this post on Facebook® Robert Garcia 15-Minute Meeting

- For SEO, Moz and Ahrefs have excellent tools and educational content to improve your podcast's search engine ranking. I recommend Patrick Burt to do the heavy lifting.

Remember, marketing and promotion are ongoing processes.

It's about building relationships with your audience and continuously finding new ways to engage and grow your listener base.

With persistence and creativity, your podcast can reach new heights.

If you have any questions contact me via email.

Chapter 8

Chapter 8: Engaging Your Audience...

Engaging your audience is a crucial element in building a loyal and interactive community. Remember: Intention, Attention, and Retention.

This chapter will guide you through practical strategies to encourage listener interaction, effectively utilize feedback and reviews, and host successful Q&A sessions or live events.

These steps are designed to foster a deeper connection with your audience and to enhance your content's impact.

Remember: people buy from those they know, like, and trust.

Encouraging Listener Interaction...

1. Ask Open-Ended Questions...

Prompt your audience with thought-provoking questions related to your content. NEVER just ask a yes or no question.

Spotify lets you create a poll in each episode you release.

This can be done through social media posts, during podcasts, or in your video content.

2. Create Interactive Content...

Develop polls, surveys, or quizzes to engage your audience actively.
I do a post everyday on Facebook® to keep my audience engaged.

These tools provide not only interaction, but also valuable insights into your audience's preferences and opinions.

3. Utilize Social Media...

Use platforms like Instagram®, Twitter now know as X, LinkedIn®, Tik-Tok®, and Facebook® to create a community space.

Facebook® and LinkedIn® are my go-to platforms.

Regularly post interactive content, such as stories or tweets, to encourage audience responses.

4. Offer Incentives…

Host contests or giveaways where audience participation is required.

We give our 2X Top-Selling Book away for free not only as a bonus gift, but to also capture their email address and build our mailing list,

This not only boosts interaction but also rewards your audience for their engagement.

Section 2: Utilizing Feedback and Reviews…

1. Create a Feedback System…

Establish a simple and accessible way for your audience to provide feedback.

This could be a form on your website, a comment section, or direct messaging on social media. Dm Is preferred!

2. Acknowledge and Respond to Feedback…

Regularly read and respond to the feedback.

I spend my first two hours of every day engaging with my audience to help build generational relationships.

Acknowledging both positive and negative comments shows that you value your audience's opinions.

This goes especially for negative comments. This helps you to find out why they feel negative about your content and what you can do to improve it.

3. Implement Changes Based on Feedback…

Show your audience that their input matters, by making changes or adjustments to your content based on their suggestions.

4. Share Testimonials and Reviews…

Highlight positive reviews and testimonials in your content or on your platforms.

Social proof is the best form of marketing you can have.

I can shout from the roof top how great I am but when Dean Graziosi shouts us out, it's a big deal.

This not only builds credibility, but also encourages others to engage and provide feedback.

Section 3: Hosting Q&A Sessions or Live Events…

1. Plan and Promote Your Event…

Choose a platform for your live event or Q&A session, such as Instagram® Live, YouTube® Live, or a webinar tool.

We use Streamyard for live events.

Promote the event ahead of time through your channels to ensure a good turnout.

2. Prepare Content in Advance…

Have a list of topics or questions ready to guide the session.

Be prepared to address common questions or areas of interest for your audience.

3. Encourage Real-Time Interaction…

During the event, actively encourage participation. Using their NAMES — their favorite subject! LOL!

Ask for questions, opinions, or experiences related to the topic at hand.

4. Follow-Up Post-Event…

After the event, share key takeaways or a summary on your platforms.

Follow up is everything!

This not only caters to those who missed the live event but also extends the lifespan of the content created during the session.

Conclusion…

Engaging your audience is a dynamic and ongoing process.

By encouraging interaction, valuing feedback, and hosting live events, you create a vibrant community around your content.

This chapter provides actionable steps to deepen your connection with your audience, enhancing both their experience and your contents's effectiveness.

As always you can reach out me via email at verticalmomentumpodcast@gmail.com.

Chapter 9

Chapter 9: Scaling and Expanding

As your podcast grows, it becomes crucial to explore avenues for scaling and expanding your reach.

This chapter will delve into effective strategies for networking with fellow podcasters, attending industry events and conferences, and venturing into cross-media opportunities.

By the end of this chapter, you will have a clear roadmap to elevate your podcast to new heights. Vertical Momentum — the only way to go is up!

Networking with Other Podcasters...

Why Network?...

Your network is your net worth.

Networking with other podcasters is not just about growing your audience; it's about building a community, learning from others' experiences, and creating opportunities for collaboration.

For some reason a lot of podcasters do not want to hang with other podcasters.

I believe in collaboration not competition.

How to Network Effectively...

1. Join Podcasting Forums and Groups...

Platforms like Reddit's r/podcasting or Facebook® groups are great places to start.

Engage actively by asking questions, sharing your experiences, and offering advice.

Always add value first before asking for anything.

2. Podcast Guest Exchanges...

Offer to be a guest on other podcasts and invite others to yours. We will be on over 200 podcasts this year.

This mutual exchange benefits both parties by tapping into each other's audiences.

3. Social Media Engagement...

Connect with fellow podcasters on platforms like X (formerly Twitter) and Instagram®.

Regular engagement can lead to meaningful connections. Remember to be social on social media!

Attending Industry Events and Conferences…

The Importance of Industry Events…

Events and conferences are not only about learning new trends and skills but also about making connections that can lead to collaborations and sponsorships.

I have made so many lifelong friends at conferences and trade shows, Some of my best friends I met at MICDC! (Military Influencer Conference, most recently in DC).

Key Events to Consider…

1. Podcast Movement…

This is the largest gathering of podcasters worldwide. Perfect for networking and learning. For more info, click here: Podcast Movement.

2.Podfest Expo…

A community-oriented event that focuses on helping podcasters of all skill levels. Learn more by clicking here: Podfest Expo

3. Local Meet-ups…

Don't overlook local events and meet-ups. They are great for building a strong local network.

Interview local leaders and influencers in your market remember your local market is your warm market.

Exploring Cross-Media Opportunities…

Expanding Beyond Podcasting…

Exploring other media like YouTube or blogging can significantly increase your podcast's visibility.

Just remember that people consume content differently. I watch YouTube®, read books, and listen to audio books to learn.

Strategies for Cross-Media Expansion…

1. YouTube®…

Start by creating videos related to your podcast content.

It could be as simple as uploading podcast recordings with static images or as complex as full-fledged video podcasts. To Get started with YouTube®, click here: YouTube

Also remember that YouTube® is the second biggest search engine in the world; and it's also owned by Google.

2. Blogging…

Create a blog where you can post episode transcripts, additional information, and related content.

Platforms like WordPress or Medium are user-friendly options, but there are many others as well.

3. Social Media Clips…

Share short, engaging clips from your podcast on platforms like Instagram® or TikTok® to attract a broader audience. Short form video is king at the time of this writing.

By implementing these strategies, you're well on your way to scaling and expanding your podcast.

Remember, the key to growth is not only in reaching more people but in building meaningful relationships and diversifying your content.

Keep experimenting; and don't be afraid to try new things. Your podcast's next level of success is just around the corner!

Reach out to us if you EVER have any questions at Vertical Momentum Podcast.

Chapter 10

Chapter 10: Course Conclusion…

Recap of Key Learnings…

Hope y'all have gotten some great knowledge from this course, as always the podcast game is always changing if you have any further questions reach out to at Vertical Momentum Podcast.

Identifying Your Niche…

Probably the most important thing I teach is how to "niche down till it hurts". As my mentor John Lee Dumas says "Go An Inch Wide But A Mile Deep", when finding your perfect avatar.

Focus on what you are passionate and knowledgeable about.

Consider the needs and interests of your target audience.

Crafting Your Podcast Format…

Choose between solo, co-hosted, or interview formats.

Determine the length and frequency of your episodes.

There is NO perfect length or frequency but you must be consistent.

Technical Setup…
Invest in quality recording equipment (microphones, headphones, recording software).

Understand the basics of sound editing and mixing.

You don't need the best equipment to start, remember some of Gary Vee's most downloaded episodes were shot on a flip-cam!

Content Creation and Planning…
Develop a content calendar.

I use the Tactical CEQ Business Visibility Planner By Dr.Rob Garcia.

Plan your episodes in advance to maintain consistency.

Building Your Audience…

Utilize social media, SEO, and community engagement.

We are on over 30 different social media platforms.

Collaborate with other podcasters and influencers. This is the fastest way to build your audience,

Monetizing Your Podcast…

Explore avenues like sponsorships, advertisements, and merchandise.

Affiliate marketing is a HUGE part of our business model.

Consider premium content offerings for loyal listeners.

Action Plan for Starting a Podcast…

Define Your Podcast's Purpose and Audience…

Write down what your podcast is about and who it is for, like Jim Rohn said "If You're Marketing To Everyone, You're Marketing To No One."

Set Up Your Recording Environment…

Acquire the necessary equipment, Amazon is your best friend.

Find a quiet and comfortable space for recording.

Record and Edit Your Pilot Episode…

Test your setup with a pilot episode.

Edit for clarity and engagement.

Launch and Promote…

Choose a hosting platform and upload your first episode. Just DO It!

Announce your podcast launch on social media and other channels, and tag all your real friends to start a street team,

Engage and Grow…

Request feedback from early listeners and put their feedback to use quickly.

Use these insights to refine future episodes.

Resources for Further Learning…

Podcast Tutorials and Courses…

Podcast Insights - Comprehensive guides on starting and growing a podcast.

Equipment Reviews and Recommendations…

The Podcast Host - Reviews of the latest podcasting gear.

Sound on Sound - Professional advice on audio equipment.

Community Forums and Support…

r/podcasting on Reddit - A community for podcasting discussions and advice.

Podcaster's Support Group on Facebook® - Networking and support group for podcasters.

Books on Podcasting…

"Podcast Launch" by John Lee Dumas: A step-by-step guide to launching your podcast.

"Out on the Wire: The Storytelling Secrets of the New Masters of Radio" by Jessica Abel: Insights into narrative and storytelling in podcasting.

In conclusion, starting a successful and profitable podcast requires a blend of passion, planning, and persistence.

Use the resources and action plan outlined in this chapter as your roadmap to launching and growing your podcast.

Remember, the journey of podcasting is as rewarding as the destination. So embrace the learning process and enjoy connecting with your audience. Happy podcasting!

Chapter 11

Chapter 11: Bonus Materials…

In this chapter, we delve into the treasure trove of additional resources that complement the primary content of our podcasting ebook.

These bonus materials are designed to give you a hands-on, practical approach to podcasting, leveraging the insights and strategies of seasoned podcasters.

From actionable checklists and customizable templates to exclusive interviews and community support, we've curated these extras to help you navigate your podcasting journey with greater ease and confidence.

Checklists and Templates..,.

Podcast Launch Checklist…

This comprehensive checklist ensures you have all bases covered for a successful podcast launch.

From initial concept development to the final launch phase, it guides you through each step with detailed instructions.

Download the Podcast Launch Checklist… https://claricast.com/podcast-launch-checklist/

Episode Planning Template…

Planning your episodes is crucial for maintaining consistency and delivering value to your listeners.

This template helps you outline your episodes, including topic selection, guest interviews, and key takeaways.

Access the Episode Planning Template… https://milanote.com/templates/podcasting

Marketing and Promotion Plan…

A strategic approach to marketing and promotion can significantly increase your podcast's reach and listener base.

his plan includes tactics for social media promotion, email marketing, and cross-promotion with other podcasters.

Get the Marketing and Promotion Plan… https://www.ausha.co/

Interviews with Successful Podcasters…

Gain insights from the experts who have made their mark in the podcasting world.

These interviews cover a range of topics, from finding your niche and building an audience to monetization strategies and overcoming challenges.

Finding Your Voice:

Watch the Interview with Sean Douglas Podcast Host, Producer, TedX Speaker discussing how to find and refine your unique voice in podcasting.

Audience Growth Tactics…

John Lee Dumas, creator of **"Entrepreneurs On Fire"** shares (on my poscast) his top growth strategies for building and engaging a podcast audience.

Monetization Mastery…

Learn Monetization Tips from John Lee Dumas who turned their podcast into a profitable venture, about the different ways to monetize your podcast effectively.

Access to our 3P'S Facebook® Community…

Join our exclusive "Purpose, Power, Profit - 3P'S Podcasting Success" Facebook® community, a vibrant group of podcasters ranging from beginners to pros.

This platform allows you to connect, share experiences, ask questions, and receive feedback from fellow podcast enthusiasts.

Networking Opportunities…

Connect with podcasters worldwide to collaborate, share resources, and support each other's growth.

Live Q&A Sessions…

Participate in live Q&A sessions with podcasting experts, gaining direct access to professional advice and tips.

Resource Sharing…

Benefit from a wealth of shared resources, including additional templates, guides, and tools recommended by community members.

As indicated above, join the 3P'S Facebook® Community…

This chapter provides you with a wealth of resources to complement the knowledge and strategies outlined in our podcasting ebook.

By leveraging these bonus materials, you can enhance your podcasting journey, from conception to growth and monetization.

Remember, the journey to podcasting success is continuous, and these resources will help you stay on track and achieve your goals.

Welcome To Your Future!

Acknowledgments

First of all, I'd like to thank God for bringing me through all my trials and tribulations.

I'd like to thank my bride, Michele, and our three beautiful children: Sean, Liam, and Linda.

I'd like to thank my Uncle Bob and Aunt Sara.

To my cousins Gina and Andrea, I love you like sisters.

I'd like to thank my best friend, Jason. Love you, bro.
I would like to thank my mentors.

As a child, I wished I would have listened more.

As I get older, I miss my Uncle Bob Robert L. Foglia more than ever.

My Uncle Tino was an amazing man who loved me when I was unlovable.

Last, but not least, my thanks to my partner-in-crime Kumar, who taught me how to be a businessman.

Thank You John Lee Dumas for mentoring me.
I would like to thank all my business mentors: Matt Matorian, Mark Dudek, Daniel Curry, Tammi Moses, Kurt Ballash, Robert Garcia, Sean Douglas, Marshall Gillen, and Donnie Boivin, for starting this whole thing.

Thank you, Trish Leto, Tucker Bearden, Patrick Mudge. Thank you, Joshua Nicholas Costner, Erik Allen, Joe Graham, Zach J Babcock, Travis Johnson, and Steven Eugene Kuhn, for pushing me to finish this project.

I know I am forgetting some people. I just want to thank all my friends and family for everything you have ever done for me. I am truly a blessed man."

Richard Kaufman
Host and Producer
www.verticalmomentumpodcast.com

THE PODCASTING BLUEPRINT: MASTERING PURPOSE, POWER AND PROFIT..

"In 'The 3P's of Podcasting - Purpose, Power, and Profit,' Richard masterfully navigates the intricate world of podcasting, offering readers an unparalleled guide to not just starting a podcast, but transforming it into a vessel of true impact, authority, and financial success.

Having witnessed his journey and growth in the podcasting realm, I can attest to the authenticity, depth, and value this book brings to all levels of podcasters.

Whether you're just contemplating the idea of starting your podcast or looking to elevate an existing one, this book provides actionable strategies, insightful anecdotes, and a clear path to harnessing the true potential of your voice.

It's a testament to the power of purpose-driven content creation, the magic of authentic engagement, and the tangible rewards of dedication.

A must-read for anyone serious about making a mark in the podcasting world."

John Lee Dumas, Host Of Entrepreneurs on Fire Podcast

www.ingramcontent.com/pod-product-compliance
Lightning Source LLC
Chambersburg PA
CBHW040138150726
48005CB00015B/2553